NES® Assessment of Professional Knowledge Secondary
National Evaluation Series™
By: Preparing Teachers In America™

This page is intentionally left blank.

© 2016 by Preparing Teachers In America

Publication by Preparing Teachers In America Publication Services, a division of Preparing Teachers In America

Printed in the United States of America

ISBN-13: 978-1540402394

ISBN-10: 1540402398

No institutions (public or private) have permission to reproduce (in any form) the contents of this publication.

This page is intentionally left blank.

Free Online Email Tutoring Services

All preparation guides purchased directly from Preparing Teachers In America includes a free three month email tutoring subscription. Any resale of preparation guides does not qualify for a free email tutoring subscription.

What is Email Tutoring?

Email Tutoring allows buyers to send questions to tutors via email. Buyers can send any questions regarding the exam processes, strategies, content questions, or practice questions.
Preparing Teachers In America reserves the right not to answer questions with or without reason(s).

How to use Email Tutoring?

Buyers need to send an email to info@preparingteachersinamerica.com requesting email tutoring services. Buyers may be required to confirm the email address used to purchase the preparation guide or additional information prior to using email tutoring. Once email tutoring subscription is confirmed, buyers will be provided an email address to send questions to. The three month period will start the day the subscription is confirmed.
Any misuse of email tutoring services will result in termination of service. Preparing Teachers In America reserves the right to terminate email tutoring subscription at anytime with or without notice.

Comments and Suggestions
All comments and suggestions for improvements for the study guide and email tutoring services need to be sent to info@preparingteachersinamerica.com.

This page is intentionally left blank.

Table of Content

This page is intentionally left blank.

About the Exam and Study Guide

What is the Assessment of Professional Knowledge Secondary Exam?

The Assessment of Professional Knowledge Secondary Exam is an exam to test potential teachers' competencies in pedagogy and professional responsibilities. The exam covers general knowledge related to planning, instructing, and assessing school students. The exam is based largely on teacher preparation standards, and the following are content areas:
- Designing Instruction and Assessment to Promote Student Learning
- Creating a Positive, Productive Classroom Environment
- Implementing Effective, Responsive Instruction and Assessment
- Fulfilling Professional Roles and Responsibilities

The Assessment of Professional Knowledge Secondary is timed at 3 hours and consists of 100 select-response questions and two constructed-response questions.

What topics are covered on the exam?

The following are some topics covered on the exam:

- instructional design and planning

- student-centered learning environments

- instructional delivery

- assessment strategies

- continuous professional improvement

- code of conduct and ethics

- teaching English Language Learners and diverse students

- literacy strategies across curriculum

What is included in this study guide book?

This guide includes one full length practice exam for the Assessment of Professional Knowledge Secondary Exam along with detail explanations. The recommendation is to take the exams under exam conditions and a quiet environment.

This page is intentionally left blank.

Exam Answer Sheet

Below is an optional answer sheet to use to document answers.

Question Number	Selected Answer	Question Number	Selected Answer	Question Number	Selected Answer	Question Number	Selected Answer
1		26		51		76	
2		27		52		77	
3		28		53		78	
4		29		54		79	
5		30		55		80	
6		31		56		81	
7		32		57		82	
8		33		58		83	
9		34		59		84	
10		35		60		85	
11		36		61		86	
12		37		62		87	
13		38		63		88	
14		39		64		89	
15		40		65		90	
16		41		66		91	
17		42		67		92	
18		43		68		93	
19		44		69		94	
20		45		70		95	
21		46		71		96	
22		47		72		97	
23		48		73		98	
24		49		74		99	
25		50		75		100	

This page is intentionally left blank.

Practice Exam Questions

QUESTION 1

Mr. James, an English teacher, is selecting instructional materials to satisfy curriculum requirements and to ensure instructional improvement. To achieve this, Mr. James should primary consider which of the following?

    A. availability of materials
    B. students' strengths and weaknesses
    C. significance of materials to goals
    D. students' past year performance

Answer:

QUESTION 2

Carlos is a nonnative speaker of English and attends high school. He is making extremely slow progress in acquiring communicative competency in English. He only communicates short phrases or writes short phrases. In addition, he has to reference a bilingual dictionary when faced with unknown words, even when context clue strategies can be used to find meaning. Carlos's teacher needs to design instruction that will prompt the development of which of the following to support Carlos's acquisition of English?

    A. grammar knowledge
    B. speaking abilities
    C. language automaticity
    D. language transfer

Answer:

QUESTION 3

A high school teacher wants her students to develop on classroom goals; the best way to promote that is by

    A. assisting students with constructing goals.
    B. watching a video about setting goals.
    C. having students set goals that they used with their teacher from last year.
    D. having students set goals and track progress on achieving those goals

Answer:

QUESTION 4

A child is coming into the classroom next year that is legally blind. What should the teacher request before the upcoming school year?

    A. manipulative
    B. communication board
    C. speakers
    D. smart board

Answer:

QUESTION 5

Which of the following situations would be most appropriate for a middle school teacher to use norm-referenced testing?

    A. decide if a student should be promoted to the next grade level
    B. decide if a group is ready to move to the next activity
    C. to confirm a diagnosis regarding special needs
    D. identify strengths and weaknesses of students

Answer:

QUESTION 6

Which of the following is the first step in choosing a new arrangement for a classroom, where students often hit into one another when they are going to the pencil sharpener, trashcan, or the water fountain?

    A. inform students not to walk too much in the classroom
    B. check for traffic patterns in the room
    C. consider the physical environment requirements for different activities
    D. look at other classroom arrangements in the school

Answer:

QUESTION 7

To ensure effective differentiation of instruction in an inclusion classroom, a teacher must first

    A. review students' IEPs.
    B. identify the needs of all students.
    C. observe students during the first few weeks.
    D. have multiple lessons that target different needs.

Answer:

QUESTION 8

If a teacher wants to make a classroom have a more student-centered environment, where should the teacher place the students' desks?

    A. back of the room
    B. front of the room
    C. center of the room
    D. side of the room

Answer:

E

QUESTION 9

Mrs. Anna, a middle-school teacher, is seeking to integrate technology in different subjects. Which of the following is the best action to take to integrate technology in the classrooms?

    A. participate in conferences
    B. participate in improvement meetings
    C. stay current on classroom technology
    D. start a blog about integration of technology in classroom

Answer:

QUESTION 10

A teacher posts something offensive in the teachers' lounge for the first time. Which of the following is the likely consequence?

    A. ban from going into the lounge
    B. termination
    C. letter of reprimand
    D. suspension

Answer:

QUESTION 11

Which of the following is the primary purpose of scaffolding student learning?

    A. ensure student learning
    B. assist students to become independent learners
    C. encourage positive group engagement
    D. assist students in independently completing assessment

Answer:

QUESTION 12

An open school event is being held at a high school. Which of the following is the most effective strategy for showing respect to and sensitivity to the cultural diversity among the families?

    A. have staff to translate for necessary families
    B. have written communication in multiple languages
    C. have staff to support students with disabilities
    D. have student-made posters of different cultures around the school

Answer:

QUESTION 13

A middle school teacher is looking to establish a positive environment between two students who have been calling each other names. Which of the following is the best first step for the teacher to undertake?

    A. have the two students participate in a paired reading activity
    B. have the two students do introductions about themselves
    C. have the two students communicate why there are calling each other names
    D. have the two students sit next to each other in the classroom

Answer:

QUESTION 14

Mr. Midwest is a ninth-grade math teacher. He was asked by the English teacher to do an integrated lesson as a part of the new curriculum. Mr. Midwest refused to do an integrated lesson. Which of the following is the best action for the English teacher to undertake?

    A. inform the school principal of Mr. Midwest's unwillingness to do an integrated lesson
    B. engage with Mr. Midwest to understand his reasoning for refusing to do integrated lesson
    C. remind Mr. Midwest that integrated lessons are a part of the new curriculum
    D. wait a week and then ask Mr. Midwest again to do an integrated lesson as a part of the new curriculum

Answer:

QUESTION 15

In the first week of school, a sixth-grade teacher asks her students to write their favorite books, movies, places, games, and foods. At the end of the day, the teacher asks students to discuss the list and provide more details. The teacher engages students to identify peers who share some common interests. The teacher also explains the importance of people being alike and different. Which of the following is the main reason for undertaking this activity?

A. promoting positive relationships within the classroom
B. promoting a community atmosphere based on common understanding and appreciation
C. helping students understand that individuals are not all the same
D. helping students identify friends in the classroom

Answer:

QUESTION 16

Which of the following is a type of test score that indicates a student's relative position among a group of students in the same grade who are tested at the same time?

A. raw score
B. average score
C. percentile rank
D. composite score

Answer:

QUESTION 17

A middle school teacher confirms that a student copied from the encyclopedia for his essay. What is the first action the teacher should take?

A. inform the parents
B. copy the essay into a plagiarism detection software
C. ask the student the method used to do the report
D. have the student redo the essay

Answer:

QUESTION 18

Which of the following is the least effective way for middle school students to learn content?

A. lecture
B. cooperative learning
C. direct instruction
D. modeling

Answer:

QUESTION 19

The teacher asks the students to close their eyes and imagine that they are in a trip by the country side. Then, he asks the students to open their eyes, and he asks questions to the students. Which strategy is the teacher using?

A. brainstorming
B. modeling
C. activating prior knowledge
D. teacher-center activity

Answer:

QUESTION 20

In the beginning of the school year, the students in an eighth-grade class have been difficult to manage, so the teacher decides to divide the class into two groups. A group receives a check mark whenever a student in the group breaks a classroom rule, and the group with the least check marks receives a privilege. If both groups receive less than a predetermined number of check marks, both are granted the privilege. This strategy is likely to be effective primarily because it takes advantage of adolescents' inclination to:

A. be more accepting to take risks than when they were younger
B. declare their independence from adult power
C. feel strongly supportive of their peers
D. act in ways that will meet with their peers' approval.

Answer:

QUESTION 21

An eighth grade teacher is worried that several students seem bored in class. Which of the following would most likely result in improvements in students' attitude toward learning?

    A. tailor lessons to students' needs
    B. connect lessons to everyday activities
    C. provide incentives for engaging
    D. have students sign learning contract

Answer:

QUESTION 22

At the end of the unit on laws of motion, Mr. Locke is seeking to determine what the students have learned. Which of the following assessments is the best to implement?

    A. authentic assessment
    B. standards-based assessment
    C. summative assessment
    D. norm-referenced assessment

Answer:

QUESTION 23

There are multiple English learners at various levels of language proficiency in a science class. The teacher displays a list of vocabulary words related to plants. Which of the following strategies will best support the English learners understanding of the words related to soccer?

    A. have students look of the meaning of each word
    B. review the words with the students
    C. imitate the words with the class
    D. model the pronunciation of the words

Answer:

QUESTION 24

Which of the following changes would be best for a tenth grade student enrolled in a regular classroom who has been diagnosed as having a writing disorder?

    A. give a concrete reinforcement for progressive improvement in handwriting legibility
    B. give the student additional handwriting practice
    C. allow the student to have digital recordings of class lectures and copies of class notes
    D. give the student the opportunity to redo work for improvement purposes

Answer:

QUESTION 25

Mr. Barry, a high school teacher, has a goal to develop an effective set of behavior expectations for students, including incentives and consequences. Which of the following guidelines will support Mr. Barry in reaching the goal?

    A. two to four general standards that channel productive learning
    B. five to ten standards that includes detailed information
    C. five to ten standards that define consequences
    D. two to four standards that engages students in doing homework

Answer:

QUESTION 26

Which of the following is the best action to take when a student with epilepsy has a seizure?

    A. stay calm and stay with the student until the seizure stops
    B. get the kids out of the room and get help
    C. stay calm, use a tongue suppressor
    D. remove any surrounding objects that can hurt the student

Answer:

QUESTION 27

Mr. Simon has a great amount of information on students' grade. He does not want to calculate the student's grade every time he is asked about grades. What is the best program he can use to support him?

    A. spreadsheet
    B. database
    C. simulation
    D. model

Answer:

QUESTION 28

A teacher surveys students about their interests in subject areas; the students' responses matter because they are?

    A. relevant
    B. valid
    C. measurable
    D. consistent

Answer:

QUESTION 29

In Mr. Cole's classroom a new student feels unfamiliar. What can Mr. Cole do so the student can feel safe in the classroom?

    A. seat the student near the quietest part of the classroom
    B. seat the student near a group that does not change position
    C. seat the student in the back of the classroom
    D. seat the student in the front of the classroom

Answer:

QUESTION 30

Prior to the start of the school year, the principal of a middle school assigns 115 students to a seventh-grade teaching team. The team must then divide the students among the five teachers. Which of the following would be the best approach for the teachers to use in making the groups?

    A. using information from students' records to create groups who are likely to function well together
    B. reviewing students' grades and test scores to create groups of students with alike ability levels
    C. giving students the opportunity on the first day of school to self-select the group
    D. randomly assigning every fifth student from an alphabetical list to the same group

Answer:

QUESTION 31

Which activity can a history teacher best use to strengthen tenth-grade students skill in another subject area while developing history knowledge?

    A. playing modern music softly while students complete history paper
    B. request students to write an essay on the theme of Rights and Responsibilities
    C. have students watch a video on the American Revolution and answer multiple choice questions
    D. asking students to read paragraphs from the Declaration of Independence and the Articles of Confederation

Answer:

QUESTION 32

In evaluating a distribution of students' test scores, the mode is determined by identifying the score that:

A. is earned by the greatest number of times by the students who took the test
B. represents the average of all scores
C. is midway between the highest and lowest scores
D. represents the 30th percentile of all scores in the set of test scores

Answer:

QUESTION 33

A high school teacher uses a systematic approach to instruction by giving detailed instructions and requirements for nearly all assignments. Which of the following is a likely consequence of this approach?

A. maximizing students' learning in the subject area
B. reducing students' ownership and responsibility in learning
C. reducing the number of mistakes made by students
D. having a better ability to see learning patterns

Answer:

QUESTION 34

A high school science teacher's goal is to get students to follow safety guidelines without constant teacher intervention during experiments. During experiments, the teacher starts by discussing the safety procedures. Which of the following additional approaches would best support the teacher to ensure accomplishment of the goal?

A. have posters in the classroom about the importance of safety procedures
B. give the students ample opportunities to implement safety procedures and receive feedback
C. give extra points for students who follow safety procedures without intervention
D. establish a buddy system to get peers to support in following safety procedures

Answer:

QUESTION 35

Matt is a sixth-grade student, and his teacher is having him collect samples of his work for a portfolio. Sample work includes the following:

- artwork
- projects
- graphs
- writing samples

The teacher engages with Matt regularly to assist him in selecting pieces for his portfolio. Which of the following is the main reason for such a portfolio?

A. support the teacher in assigning report card grades
B. show parents of the work being done in class
C. support the student in seeing academic progress
D. show effectiveness of teaching strategies

Answer:

QUESTION 36

Mr. Locke, a high school teacher, is teaching a science lesson on the laws of motion. He knows that his students have a natural understanding of the topic going into it. He is intending to understand what they know before he begins the unit. He will use their prior knowledge to create activities to help them understand the physical laws. Which of the following assessments is best for Mr. Locke?

A. criterion-based assessment
B. norms-based assessment
C. formative assessment
D. authentic assessment

Answer:

QUESTION 37

    I.   coming to school very irritable
    II.   being hyperactive most of the day
    III. fighting with other children

The first step the teacher needs to take in this situation is to:

    A. refer the student to the school nurse for deficit/hyperactivity disorder symptoms
    B. monitor the behavior for few months to discuss with the principal
    C. discuss with parents on home behavior
    D. engage with the administrator to develop an intervention plan to support the student

Answer:

QUESTION 38

A student and a teacher analyze one novel together by looking at its plot, setting, and characters. Afterward, the teacher asks the student to read three different novels to compare the plots, settings, and characters. What is the objective of this activity?

    A. understand vocabulary
    B. increase reading fluency
    C. promote analytical thinking skills
    D. help students understand the meaning of plot, setting, and character

Answer:

QUESTION 39

An assistant principal, a principal, and grade level teachers are getting together to discuss math scores to improve scores for the following school year. What kind of meeting are they holding?

    A. school improvement planning
    B. grade level planning
    C. teacher development planning
    D. district improvement planning

Answer:

QUESTION 40

Which of the following types of assessments includes a variety of samples of a student's work, collected overtime, that shows the student's growth and development?

    A. anecdotal records
    B. portfolio
    C. running record
    D. grades

Answer:

QUESTION 41

Mr. Mark has a student that has been diagnosed with a disease, and the student will be missing school frequently. The student is in the process of being tested to confirm the prognosis. In class, Mr. Mark's best action to take is:

    A. to observe the student carefully and ask the student frequently if she is doing well
    B. to inform the student that she can go to the nurse at anytime with permission
    C. to send reports to the parents on how the student is doing during class
    D. to assist her in understanding the disease and let her know she has the support of her teacher

Answer:

QUESTION 42

_____ instruction is unambiguous and direct approach to teaching that includes both instructional design and delivery procedures, which includes series of supports or scaffolds, whereby students are guided through the learning process.

    A. Intensive instruction
    B. Indirect instruction
    C. Explicit instruction
    D. Individualized instruction

Answer:

QUESTION 43

   I.   flashcard
   II. indirect instruction
   III. paired activity
   IV. repetition

A middle school reading teacher is having the students read a short story. The teacher starts by having the students develop vocabulary words related to the short story with flashcards. Then, the teacher reads the book out loud while the students listen. After that, the teacher pairs the students, and the teacher has the students read the short story again. Which of the following planned supports did the teacher use in this activity?

   A. I and III
   B. III and IV
   C. I, III, and IV
   D. I, II, III, and IV

Answer:

QUESTION 44

A high school teacher is looking to assess the academic achievement of nonnative speakers of English with a standards-based assessment. Which of the following is the most critical aspect of a potential assessment for this purpose?

   A. exam format
   B. free of cultural and linguistic bias
   C. includes common vocabulary words
   D. includes clues to help understand complex questions

Answer:

QUESTION 45

    I.   a portfolio

    II.   an intelligence test

    III.   an adaptive behavior scale

Of the above, which of the following is/are formal assessment(s)?

A. I and II
B. I and III
C. II and III
D. I, II, and III

Answer:

QUESTION 46

Which of the following is the most effective for a teacher to do when making classroom rules?

A. State the rules ones at the beginning of the school year.
B. Communicate the rules in an authoritative manner.
C. Post the rules on the walls of the classroom.
D. Explain the purpose of rules to better student engagement.

Answer:

QUESTION 47

An eighth-grade teacher desires to ensure active engagement for students working on an open-ended research question for an English writing paper. The best approach is to use

_____.

A. formal assessments
B. inquiry-based instruction
C. indirect instruction
D. explicit teaching

Answer:

QUESTION 48

More than 70% of a 3rd-grade class scored at high risk on the oral reading fluency. Which instructional practice would be best for improving the students' oral reading fluency?

    A. having students independently read
    B. having students participate in round-robin reading
    C. having students repeat readings of familiar text with corrective feedback
    D. having students do a paired-reading activity

Answer:

QUESTION 49

In gym class, James is unable to walk across a balance beam. Which of the following is the best option to undertake?

    A. place tape next to the beam and have him walk on the tape
    B. defer activity to the latter part of the year
    C. have him write how others completed activity
    D. have him watch video of kids walking across a balance beam

Answer:

QUESTION 50

A teacher starts developing a lesson plan by deciding the instructional outcomes. The most appropriate next step for the teacher to take in planning the lesson is to determine

    A. the activities that should be included.
    B. the assessment type for the activity.
    C. the resources required in the lesson.
    D. if the outcome is realistic for the grade level.

Answer:

QUESTION 51

An ESL teacher teaches beginning-level English Language Learners conversational techniques such as elaboration and circumlocution. To allow students to apply the techniques, the teacher has the students practice these strategies in conversations with partners at different English proficiency levels. The teacher's instructional method primarily allows the students' to develop by

- A. increasing relationship with classmates.
- B. giving opportunity to produce logical language output.
- C. allowing students to see different levels of English proficiency.
- D. giving students opportunity to apply knowledge.

Answer:

QUESTION 52

Which of the following best represents a commitment from teachers, parents, and students to work together to support student learning?

- A. parent teacher conference
- B. learning contract
- C. progress report
- D. letter informing expectations

Answer: B

QUESTION 53

Which statement would be classified as a long term goal rather than a course or lesson objective?

- A. The student will analyze independently informational text.
- B. The student will be able to identify the verbs in a paragraph.
- C. The student will be able to develop a well organized presentation.
- D. The student will be able to identify main ideas.

Answer:

QUESTION 54

Daryl is concerned about one of his eleventh grade student who has missed many school days recently. When Daryl approached the student with his concern, the student informed him that school was not worth going to and saw no need to pursue school so he was working at a part-time restaurant. In order to understand the student's perspective, Daryl needs to have which development knowledge to pursue forward in an effective dialogue?

    A. The student may have financial difficulties at home.
    B. The student may not have any concern for the future and is more concerned with the present.
    C. The student is likely still operating at the operational stage of thinking process.
    D. Students at this age typically place more focus on peer modeling.

Answer:

QUESTION 55

A ninth grade teacher has her students participate in a series of debates on school related topics. Topics include dress code and afterschool programs. This activity is related to ninth grade student mostly because students at this age have typically developed the ability to

    A. establish good communication skills to debate.
    B. perceive different perspectives on issues.
    C. think at higher level.
    D. engage in formal operational thinking.

Answer:

QUESTION 56

A teacher is planning to organize study teams for the entire school year in order for students to support other students. Prior to assigning the groups, the teacher undertakes the following:

1. Observes students interaction in various team activities
2. Gives some homework and grade the homework
3. Gives explicit instructions on how study teams function

The approach taken by the teacher in developing study team is expected to benefit the student most by:

A. having groups organized to ensure no one student is working more than the other
B. establishing a network of peers who can support one another
C. increasing communication and collaborating skills
D. increase student attention and seriousness of school

Answer:

QUESTION 57

A high school physics teacher is on the lesson of velocity and acceleration. The teacher has done the following to convey information to the students:

- discussed relevant sections from textbook
- created diagrams to explain the concepts
- shown videos on velocity and acceleration applications in science

After completing the above, the students are still having difficulty understanding the concept related to velocity and acceleration. Which of the following is the most appropriate to undertake next to assist in students' understanding these concepts?

A. explain basics behind velocity and acceleration
B. repeat the information, but take breaks to ask questions for understanding
C. provide students with examples of the concepts related to their own experiences
D. perform experiments that explain velocity and acceleration

Answer:

QUESTION 58

An eighth-grade teacher is going to have her class undertake an individual research project in which students will be required to write a paper on a self-selected topic. Later, he teacher decides to have students complete the research paper in small groups. Which of the following is a reason explaining why the group approach is going to be most effective for eighth-grade students?

   A. increase participation as students will be able to communicate with peers in learning process
   B. increase students' interests as work will be distributed
   C. allow students to complete detailed and complex research in groups
   D. give students opportunity to learn from other students on unfamiliar topics

Answer:

QUESTION 59

A teacher has been working at a school for three months. After evaluating the needs of the district, the teacher has been informed that she will have to go to another school. The teacher refuses this move, and she takes action to abandon the position without in advance notification. The teacher has:

   A. inappropriately abandon the position
   B. the right to abandon the position
   C. taken appropriate action
   D. breached the contract

Answer:

QUESTION 60

A teacher is seeking to find out if students have mastered the instructional objectives at the end of the unit. What type of assessment is the best to use?

   A. norm referenced
   B. achievement
   C. diagnostic
   D. placement

Answer:

QUESTION 61

In a middle school classroom, a student is constantly distracting students during silent reading. From the standpoint of logical consequence approach to classroom management, which of the following is the best action for the teacher to take?

    A. place the student to an individual work station during silent reading
    B. remind him that there will be consequences for interruptions
    C. have the student hear the teacher during silent reading
    D. assign a buddy to help the student stay on track

Answer:

QUESTION 62

Which of the following instructional strategies best completes the chart?

Reading Comprehension	Reading Fluency	Writing	Vocabulary
Think-Pair-Share	Readers' theater	Revision	Word walls
Direct Reading-Thinking	?	Sentence combining	Word hunts
Inquiry chart	Partner reading	Paragraph hamburger	Possible sentence

    A. Shared reading
    B. Brainstorming
    C. Anticipation guide
    D. Guided reading

Answer:

QUESTION 63

The Family Educational Rights and Privacy Act of 1974 give parents/guardians of a minor who is getting special needs services the right to:

A. remove their child from standardize exams
B. obtain educational records to share with non-school individuals
C. select special education services
D. opt out of IEP meetings

Answer:

QUESTION 64

IDEA covers which of the following disabilities from birth:

    I.   cerebral palsy
    II.   visual impairment
    III.   Down syndrome
    IV.   hearing impairment

A. I and III
B. II and IV
C. I and II
D. III and IV

Answer:

QUESTION 65

What is one way a teacher can avoid confusion and delays caused by activity transitions?

A. increase voice during transitions to ensure everyone is listening
B. establish a daily schedule with clear objectives
C. ask students to stop all work and put down their pencils
D. provide incentives for timely transitions

Answer:

QUESTION 66

Interactive writing between the student and the teacher is:

    A. dialogue journal
    B. essay writing
    C. social network
    D. unethical

Answer:

QUESTION 67

A student doesn't understand very well what the teacher is explaining. The teacher realizes that the student is having hearing loss. What kind of assistive technology can the teacher use to help the student with the problem?

    A. visuals
    B. gestures
    C. text-to-voice technology
    D. speech-to-text technology

Answer:

QUESTION 68

A reporter is interested about the social activities that a student is involved within a high school club, and asks the teacher about the student. The teacher should:

    A. tell the reporter that the student is enrolled
    B. report to the principal
    C. invite the reporter to the school
    D. not tell the reporter anything regarding the student

Answer:

QUESTION 69

Which of the following assessments is used to evaluate student learning at the conclusion of an instructional period (ex. at the end of a unit)?

A. formative assessment
B. interim assessment
C. summative assessment
D. placement assessment

Answer:

QUESTION 70

A classroom teacher consults with another teacher regarding the best approach for meeting the needs of a culturally different student who is about to enter the class. Which of the following would be the most appropriate advice?

A. reward students in the class who assist the new student.
B. adhere to current instructional programs and standards
C. provide the student with instruction in the social and cultural values of the United States
D. investigate the student's culture to improve understanding of cultural differences to improve learning

Answer:

QUESTION 71

A student panics during a fire drill and runs out of the classroom. What approach could the teacher implement to stop this from happening in the future?

A. show a video of fire drill procedures and safety rules
B. practice role playing a fire drill situation; practicing rules and procedures
C. have a discussion about rules and procedures of fire drills
D. explain the procedures for a fire drill and have the student write the procedures

Answer:

QUESTION 72

Parents come to school and want to see their child's records. The teacher should inform the parents that:

    A. they need to make an appointment to see records
    B. records are confidential and cannot be shown to anyone
    C. allow them to see the child's records
    D. have them discuss the request with the principal

Answer:

QUESTION 73

Which of the following is the best to use when deciding whether or not the students are ready for the next content?

    A. survey students to determine if they are ready to move to the next content area
    B. review progress reports and report cards
    C. review previous standardized tests
    D. administer entrance tests

Answer:

QUESTION 74

A 55% percentile rank means what?

    A. 55% of questions correct
    B. below 55%
    C. above 55%
    D. 55% better than the rest of the kids

Answer:

QUESTION 75

High school teachers meet frequently to discuss strategies to support students struggling in science. Which of the following is the main benefit of their meetings?

    A. gives opportunity to support all students
    B. provides different instructional methods
    C. provides professional development
    D. eliminates poor practices and fosters positive practices

Answer:

QUESTION 76

Mrs. Barbara is seeking to teach listening skills to her early childhood students. What is the best approach for her to take?

    A. play a guessing game
    B. call on students not participating
    C. reading different stories and having the students answer questions about the story
    D. state a list of nonsense words and have the students repeat them back

Answer:

QUESTION 77

Kate focuses better in the morning. How can Kate's teacher better instruct her?

    A. direct instruction needs to be done in the afternoon
    B. direct instruction needs to be done in the morning
    C. complete group activities in the morning
    D. teach only in the morning

Answer:

QUESTION 78

The school sent out a notice not to bring lunches with peanut butter. Jake, a middle-grade student, who has brought a peanut butter sandwich for lunch. The teacher saw the sandwich immediately, when Jake took it out of his lunch box. What should the teacher do first?

A. call the school nurse in case someone has an allergic reaction
B. take the sandwich and throw it in a trash basket away from the students
C. have Jake sit away from the students to eat his sandwich
D. call Jake's parents to remind him to not bring lunch with peanut butter

Answer:

QUESTION 79

Mr. Raymond has seen that John, who is claustrophobic, has been the last person to turn in-class assignment 12 times in a row. His grades on the assignments are above average. What is the likely reason for John being the last person to turn in assignments?

A. He double checks his work.
B. He is shy to come up to the front.
C. He does not want to come upfront while everyone else is turning in assignments.
D. He is afraid someone might push him.

Answer:

QUESTION 80

I.   all special education students in America
II. students with severe disabilities
III. students eligible for special education in public schools

IEP is/are required for:

A. I only
B. I and II
C. II and III
D. I, II, and III

Answer:

QUESTION 81

For the last two weeks, a teacher has been abruptly ending lessons as she is unable to finish teaching. The best approach is to:

   A. decrease the length of the lesson activity
   B. increase the speed of teaching
   C. have students ask questions at the very end
   D. find a way to end the lessons in a smooth manner even if the lessons are not completed

Answer:

QUESTION 82

Which of the following is the best listening comprehension content for English Learners who have mastered basic structural forms but not vocabulary development?

   A. vocabulary words to memorize
   B. oral readings with accompanying pictures
   C. television shows
   D. flashcards

Answer:

QUESTION 83

Jake, a high school math teacher, is teaching one student the entire day. Blair, a general education teacher, has observed that Jake is doing nothing to teach the student. The first action for Blair to undertake is:

   A. confront the teacher and inform the teacher to do his job
   B. inform the school principal
   C. open dialogue to see what Jake has done and continue to observe
   D. inform Jake that he can ask for support

Answer:

QUESTION 84

_____ are assessments that provide information on where an individual student's performance is in relation to his/her peers.

    A. Formative assessments
    B. Norm-referenced assessments
    C. Criterion-referenced assessments
    D. Subjective assessments

Answer:

QUESTON 85

    I.   be informed of specific charges
   II.   have character witnesses during punishment phase
 III.   have their case be heard at the district level

Students who are facing suspension for actions that violate school rules have the right to:

    A. I only
    B. I and II
    C. II and III
    D. I, II, and III

Answer:

QUESTION 86

Which of the following would be best for preparing students on taking standardized tests?

    A. Teach test-taking skills from the beginning of the year as part of regular instruction.
    B. Prior to two-three months of examination, teach test-taking skills as part of regular instruction.
    C. Devote one day of the week to teach test-taking skills.
    D. Subject area teachers should teach test-taking skills to all students.

Answer:

QUESTION 87

Which technique is most effective in promoting a ninth grade teacher's expectations for assignments?

    A. keeping a list of due dates for each assignment for the grade period
    B. maintaining a list of assignments due for each 9 week grading period
    C. requiring parent's signature on each assignment
    D. posting a grading rubrics for each assignment

Answer:

QUESTION 88

A middle school teacher is looking to use an informal assessment to capture overall learning. Which of the following is the best option?

    A. authentic assessment
    B. graded homework
    C. exit card
    D. performance assessment

Answer:

QUESTION 89

Cole, a seventh-grade student with ADHD, is not happy with his grade and is loudly communicating that to his teacher. What is the best action for the teacher to take?

    A. re-grade the assignment
    B. explain to the student what he got incorrect, so he can prevent the same mistakes in the future
    C. allow him to retake the assignment
    D. inform the student there will be more opportunities to improve

Answer:

QUESTION 90

_____ score is a measurement concept that compares a student's test performance with those of other students of the same grade level?

A. Scaled
B. Developmental
C. Standard
D. Average

Answer:

QUESTION 91

Carla is the mother of Susan, who attends middle school. Susan has come home multiple times with scratches inflicted by another student, Martha. Which of the following best indicates the most inappropriate response for the teacher to undertake along with what action the teacher should undertake?

A. The teacher would be wrong to tell the parent that Martha and Susan had difficulty working together that day. The teacher would be right in informing the parent that she will monitor both students closely going forward and report back.
B. The teacher would be wrong to generalize that there might have been some provocative verbal communication, which resulted in the scratches. The teacher would be right to take action by involving the principal and recommending appropriate punishments.
C. The teacher would be wrong to suggest that Martha's action resulted due to issues occurring in her family. The teacher would be right in informing the parent that she will monitor both students closely going forward and report back.
D. The teacher would be wrong to generalize that there might have been some provocative verbal communication, which resulted in the scratches. The teacher would be right in informing the parent that she will monitor both students closely going forward and report back.

Answer:

QUESTION 92

Mary, a middle school teacher, is alarmed by one student's appearance and behavior as the perceptions seems that she has been physically abused at home. According to state and federal law, the teacher is required to immediately:

A. inform the school nurse to allow him or her to take appropriate action
B. ensure her suspicions are reported in compliance with state/federal law requirements
C. contact the parents to inform them of the situation
D. ask indirect questions to confirm suspicions and proceed in contacting law enforcement

Answer:

QUESTION 93

Family Educational Rights and Privacy Action (FERPA) protect students' records at school institutions in America. Which of the following situations of a request to see a student's records will be approved?

A. A parent seeking to confirm a student's enrollment in the appropriate special education program.
B. A parent seeking to confirm a student's IEP is acceptable to ensure proper learning.
C. A parent questioning a student's placement for special education classes for the new school year.
D. A parent questioning a student's grades and requesting to see all assignment grades.

Answer: C

QUESTION 94

A teacher notices a student removing food from lunch and hiding it in his backpack. The teacher notices this behavior and discusses it with the student after class. In the discussion, the student mentions his father lost his job and that there is not much food to eat. Which of the following is the most appropriate first response for the teacher to take?

    A. contact the principal to develop a plan to ensure proper food is given to the student outside of the school

    B. contact Child Protective Services (CPS) to report possible neglect at home

    C. provide the student with food and snacks to take home going forward

    D. speak to the family about relevant community services and support during this difficult time

Answer:

QUESTION 95

A student brings a gift to school for his teacher. The best action for the teacher is to refuse the gift if:

    A. the gift is expensive

    B. the gift would affect student-teacher relationship

    C. the student's parents are unaware

    D. the student's gift is cheap

Answer:

QUESTION 96

Several ninth-grade students are doing well in math class, but they are having difficulty on tests and quizzes, what should their teacher do?

    A. find out their study habits and find lessons to support the students
    B. plan a unit on study habits
    C. see if there are patterns on the questions students are getting wrong
    D. do review sessions before tests and quizzes

Answer:

QUESTION 97

Juan is an eighth grade student. Coming to class every day is very important for his success in learning. The teacher notices that Juan has missed class every Thursday for the last four weeks. What is the best action for the teacher to take?

    A. ask Juan what he does on Thursday
    B. call his parents to discuss the absences
    C. have someone track Juan on Thursday
    D. tell Juan that missing class on any Thursday is unacceptable

Answer:

QUESTION 98

To prevent common cold and the flu within schools, a teacher can

    A. have students wash hands properly and frequently throughout the day
    B. have students not work in group activities
    C. discourage sharing food
    D. keep tissues near each students' desks

Answer:

QUESTION 99

The purpose of putting severely handicapped students in a general education classroom is to:

    A. teach life skills
    B. teach academic skills
    C. teach same lessons
    D. teach social skills

Answer:

QUESTION 100

James is student with a Functional Behavioral Assessment (FBA). He has unexpectedly become physically aggressive with others in school. To ensure effective intervention, which of the following should be done first by the IEP team?

    A. interview peers and teachers
    B. define behavior in measureable terms
    C. predict reasoning for changes in behavior
    D. develop a plan to collect data

Answer:

Constructed Response 1

Use the information below to complete the task that follows.

Mr. Barry is a sixth-grade math teacher whose fifth-period class includes 30 students. The class includes five students who have been identified as gifted and two students with cognitive impairment.

Mr. Barry is moving into doing advance mathematics related to operations. He is reviewing previous assessments and records of all students related to performing basic operations (addition, subtraction, multiplication, and division), which results in answers of 450 or greater.

Assessment Records – Summary			
	Score Range (% correct)	**Mean Score**	**Median Score**
Single Operations			
Addition	78-95	84	74
Subtraction	74-95	85	73
Multiplication	73-97	84	75
Division	74-95	83	73
Multiple Operations			
Addition/Subtraction	56-76	60	62
Addition/Division	63-77	70	68
Division/Multiplication	53-59	54	54
Multiplication/Subtraction	53-60	54	54

Citing evidence from the information provided, write a response in which you:

- identify one specific learning need related to the planned lesson for students in Mr. Barry's class;
- describe one strategy for differentiating instruction in the planned lesson to address the identified need; and
- explain why the strategy you described would be effective in addressing the identified need.

Constructed Response 2

Use the information below to complete the task that follows.

Mr. Martin, a sixth-grade reading teacher, has a classroom with 30 heterogeneously grouped students ages 13 to 15. The teacher is looking to start the lesson on reading factual texts. In particular, the teacher is looking to do cross curriculum lesson in which the teacher will have students read text related to World War II. Below includes information on three of Mr. Martin's students.

Student 1 – Alex

- came to America roughly one year ago
- nonnative speaker of English
- unable to respond to questions with confidence
- misspells words constantly
- barely communicates with classmates

Student 2 – Lila

- unexpectedly becomes aggressive with others
- reads at a fourth grade level
- recently diagnosed with ADHD
- always unhappy with her grade
- distracting other students

Student 3 – Jasper

- mild form of dyslexia
- recently been told by doctor to wear glasses
- fails to turn in assignments on time
- shy to answer questions in discussion
- has test anxiety

Citing evidence from the information provided, write a response in which you:

- Identify two learning supports Mr. Martin can use to support all three learners.
- Explain how the learning supports helps each of the student in learning.

This page is intentionally left blank.

Practice Exam Answers

Question Number	Selected Answer	Question Number	Selected Answer	Question Number	Selected Answer	Question Number	Selected Answer
1	C	26	D	51	B	76	D
2	C	27	A	52	B	77	B
3	A	28	A	53	A	78	B
4	C	29	B	54	B	79	C
5	C	30	A	55	B	80	C
6	B	31	B	56	B	81	D
7	B	32	A	57	C	82	B
8	D	33	B	58	A	83	C
9	B	34	B	59	D	84	B
10	C	35	C	60	B	85	A
11	B	36	C	61	A	86	B
12	A	37	D	62	A	87	D
13	C	38	C	63	B	88	C
14	C	39	A	64	A	89	B
15	B	40	B	65	B	90	C
16	C	41	A	66	A	91	C
17	C	42	C	67	D	92	B
18	A	43	C	68	D	93	C
19	A	44	B	69	C	94	D
20	D	45	C	70	D	95	B
21	B	46	D	71	B	96	A
22	C	47	B	72	C	97	B
23	C	48	C	73	D	98	A
24	C	49	A	74	B	99	D
25	A	50	D	75	A	100	B

NOTE: Getting approximately 80% of the questions correct increases chances of obtaining passing score on the real exam. This varies from different states and university programs.

This page is intentionally left blank.

Practice Exam Questions And Explanations

QUESTION 1

Mr. James, an English teacher, is selecting instructional materials to satisfy curriculum requirements and to ensure instructional improvement. To achieve this, Mr. James should primary consider which of the following?

A. availability of materials
B. students' strengths and weaknesses
C. significance of materials to goals
D. students' past year performance

Answer: C

Explanation: The keywords in the question are instructional materials, curriculum requirements, and instructional improvement. Instructional improvement indicates that goals need to be achieved when instructing students, so selecting material that have relevance to the identified goals will support fulfilling curriculum requirements and ensuring instructional improvement.

QUESTION 2

Carlos is a nonnative speaker of English and attends high school. He is making extremely slow progress in acquiring communicative competency in English. He only communicates short phrases or writes short phrases. In addition, he has to reference a bilingual dictionary when faced with unknown words, even when context clue strategies can be used to find meaning. Carlos's teacher needs to design instruction that will prompt the development of which of the following to support Carlos's acquisition of English?

A. grammar knowledge
B. speaking abilities
C. language automaticity
D. language transfer

Answer: C

Explanation: Once the student has learned language more automatically, the student will have better skills in communicating and writing.

QUESTION 3

A high school teacher wants her students to develop on classroom goals; the best way to promote that is by

    A. assisting students with constructing goals.
    B. watching a video about setting goals.
    C. having students set goals that they used with their teacher from last year.
    D. having students set goals and track progress on achieving those goals.

Answer: A

Explanation: The best answer is to support students in constructing goals. Watching a video is not going to be the most effective way as students are not involved in developing goals. Using last year's goals is not the approach to take as no new goals are established. Choice D is eliminated as the question asked about developing classroom goals; not tracking progress.

QUESTION 4

A child is coming into the classroom next year that is legally blind. What should the teacher request before the upcoming school year?

    A. manipulative
    B. communication board
    C. speakers
    D. smart board

Answer: C

Explanation: The student is blind, so the teacher should request something that will support the students learning. Since the student can hear, the best request is for speakers.

QUESTION 5

Which of the following situations would be most appropriate for a middle school teacher to use norm-referenced testing?

  A. decide if a student should be promoted to the next grade level
  B. decide if a group is ready to move to the next activity
  C. to confirm a diagnosis regarding special needs
  D. identify strengths and weaknesses of students

Answer: C

Explanation: Norm-referenced tests report whether test takers performed better or worse than the average student. From the answer choices, the most appropriate use of norm-referenced testing is to confirm a diagnosis regarding special needs. The test will confirm if the student is performing better or worse than an average student.

QUESTION 6

Which of the following is the first step in choosing a new arrangement for a classroom, where students often hit into one another when they are going to the pencil sharpener, trashcan, or the water fountain?

  A. inform students not to walk too much in the classroom
  B. check for traffic patterns in the room
  C. consider the physical environment requirements for different activities
  D. look at other classroom arrangements in the school

Answer: B

Explanation: The students will walk around the classroom, so the teacher wants to look at traffic patterns in the room to design how the classroom needs to be arranged to prevent students from hitting one another.

QUESTION 7

To ensure effective differentiation of instruction in an inclusion classroom, a teacher must first

    A. review students' IEPs.
    B. identify the needs of all students.
    C. observe students during the first few weeks.
    D. have multiple lessons that target different needs.

Answer: B

Explanation: Differentiation requires understanding the needs of the students. To ensure effective differentiation, the teacher must first identify needs of the students. Reviewing students' IEPs is a good approach, but that does not take into account students without disabilities. Observing is a good approach, but not the first step for effective differentiation. Having multiple lessons will not be best from a classroom time management standpoint.

QUESTION 8

If a teacher wants to make a classroom have a more student-centered environment, where should the teacher place the students' desks?

    A. back of the room
    B. front of the room
    C. center of the room
    D. side of the room

Answer: D

Explanation: Student-centered classrooms are big on collaboration, which means students' desks are not facing a teacher desk. Of the choices, the one that engages the students the most is with desks on the side of the room. This allows collaboration with students sitting next to each other and across from each other.

QUESTION 9

Mrs. Anna, a middle-school teacher, is seeking to integrate technology in different subjects. Which of the following is the best action to take to integrate technology in the classrooms?

    A. participate in conferences
    B. participate in improvement meetings
    C. stay current on classroom technology
    D. start a blog about integration of technology in classroom

Answer: B

Explanation: The teacher can get involved in improvement meetings and express how technology can support the classrooms. The other options do not have a greater impact or greater chances of getting technology integrated in the classrooms.

QUESTION 10

A teacher posts something offensive in the teachers' lounge for the first time. Which of the following is the likely consequence?

    A. ban from going into the lounge
    B. termination
    C. letter of reprimand
    D. suspension

Answer: C

Explanation: This is the first time the teacher has posted something offensive. The likely consequence is letter of reprimand. Termination and suspension are too harsh. Banning from the teachers' lounge is too light of a consequence.

QUESTION 11

Which of the following is the primary purpose of scaffolding student learning?

- A. ensure student learning
- B. assist students to become independent learners
- C. encourage positive group engagement
- D. assist students in independently completing assessment

Answer: B

Explanation: The purpose of scaffolding is to get students knowledgeable to allow them to independently complete activities.

QUESTION 12

An open school event is being held at a high school. Which of the following is the most effective strategy for showing respect to and sensitivity to the cultural diversity among the families?

- A. have staff to translate for necessary families
- B. have written communication in multiple languages
- C. have staff to support students with disabilities
- D. have student-made posters of different cultures around the school

Answer: A

Explanation: Having staff members translate for families with home languages other than English is the most effective strategy. This shows that the school took extra steps to ensure that information is communicated and questions are being asked by all individuals.

QUESTION 13

A middle school teacher is looking to establish a positive environment between two students who have been calling each other names. Which of the following is the best first step for the teacher to undertake?

    A. have the two students participate in a paired reading activity
    B. have the two students do introductions about themselves
    C. have the two students communicate why there are calling each other names
    D. have the two students sit next to each other in the classroom

Answer: C

Explanation: In order for the teacher to establish a positive environment, the teacher will need to know the reasons for the students' behaviors. Option B is the step to take after Option C. Option A and option D are not going to do anything in establishing a positive environment.

QUESTION 14

Mr. Midwest is a ninth-grade math teacher. He was asked by the English teacher to do an integrated lesson as a part of the new curriculum. Mr. Midwest refused to do an integrated lesson. Which of the following is the best action for the English teacher to undertake?

    A. inform the school principal of Mr. Midwest's unwillingness to do an integrated lesson
    B. engage with Mr. Midwest to understand his reasoning for refusing to do integrated lesson
    C. remind Mr. Midwest that integrated lessons are a part of the new curriculum
    D. wait a week and then ask Mr. Midwest again to do an integrated lesson as a part of the new curriculum

Answer: C

Explanation: Getting the principal involved is not the best approach to take as it might establish a difficult environment. Waiting a week and then asking again is not going to likely change Mr. Midwest's position. Engaging Mr. Midwest will give insight into why he refused, and the English teacher can remind Mr. Midwest this is a requirement. Just informing Mr. Midwest that it is a requirement of new curriculum might not be as effective as engaging.

QUESTION 15

In the first week of school, a sixth-grade teacher asks her students to write their favorite books, movies, places, games, and foods. At the end of the day, the teacher asks students to discuss the list and provide more details. The teacher engages students to identify peers who share some common interests. The teacher also explains the importance of people being alike and different. Which of the following is the main reason for undertaking this activity?

    A. promoting positive relationships within the classroom
    B. promoting a community atmosphere based on common understanding and appreciation
    C. helping students understand that individuals are not all the same
    D. helping students identify friends in the classroom

Answer: B

Explanation: The teacher is helping students identify peers who share common interest along with explaining the importance of people being alike and different. This is related to establishing a community environment with understanding that people share similarities and differences.

QUESTION 16

Which of the following is a type of test score that indicates a student's relative position among a group of students in the same grade who are tested at the same time?

    A. raw score
    B. average score
    C. percentile rank
    D. composite score

Answer: C

Explanation: A student's percentile rank indicates the percent of students in a particular group that received raw scores lower than the raw score of the student. It shows the student's relative position among a group of students.

QUESTION 17

A middle school teacher confirms that a student copied from the encyclopedia for his essay. What is the first action the teacher should take?

    A. inform the parents
    B. copy the essay into a plagiarism detection software
    C. ask the student the method used to do the report
    D. have the student redo the essay

Answer: C

Explanation: The keyword in the question is "first". Informing the parents is not the first step to take. The teacher has confirmed plagiarism has happened, so there is no need to use plagiarism detection software. Asking the student to redo the essay is a good approach but not the first step to take. Asking the student the method used to do the report is the first action to get the student to admit to cheating.

QUESTION 18

Which of the following is the least effective way for middle school students to learn content?

    A. lecture
    B. cooperative learning
    C. direct instruction
    D. modeling

Answer: A

Explanation: The least effective learning method for elementary students is lecturing as there is little interaction with the students.

QUESTION 19

The teacher asks the students to close their eyes and imagine that they are in a trip by the country side. Then, he asks the students to open their eyes, and he asks questions to the students. Which strategy is the teacher using?

    A. brainstorming
    B. modeling
    C. activating prior knowledge
    D. teacher-center activity

Answer: A

Explanation: The teacher is not modeling anything. The activity is not teacher-centered. The activity does not activate prior knowledge. The word "imagine" is an aspect of brainstorming.

QUESTION 20

In the beginning of the school year, the students in an eighth-grade class have been difficult to manage, so the teacher decides to divide the class into two groups. A group receives a check mark whenever a student in the group breaks a classroom rule, and the group with the least check marks receives a privilege. If both groups receive less than a predetermined number of check marks, both are granted the privilege. This strategy is likely to be effective primarily because it takes advantage of adolescents' inclination to:

    A. be more accepting to take risks than when they were younger
    B. declare their independence from adult power
    C. feel strongly supportive of their peers
    D. act in ways that will meet with their peers' approval.

Answer: D

Explanation: This approach groups students together, and the consequence of one student will impact everyone in the group. This will force the students to meet expectations of their peers to receive extra privileges.

QUESTION 21

An eighth grade teacher is worried that several students seem bored in class. Which of the following would most likely result in improvements in students' attitude toward learning?

    A. tailor lessons to students' needs
    B. connect lessons to everyday activities
    C. provide incentives for engaging
    D. have students sign learning contract

Answer: B

Explanation: The students are bored in the class. To get the students involved, the best way is to connect the lesson to everyday activity. Providing incentives might work to engage students, but the question is asking improvements in students' attitude toward learning. Attitude can change by connecting to students' interests and everyday activities.

QUESTION 22

At the end of the unit on laws of motion, Mr. Locke is seeking to determine what the students have learned. Which of the following assessments is the best to implement?

    A. authentic assessment
    B. standards-based assessment
    C. summative assessment
    D. norm-referenced assessment

Answer: C

Explanation: The goal of a summative assessment is to assess student learning at the end of an instructional unit by comparing it against some standards or objectives.

QUESTION 23

There are multiple English learners at various levels of language proficiency in a science class. The teacher displays a list of vocabulary words related to plants. Which of the following strategies will best support the English learners understanding of the words related to soccer?

    A. have students look of the meaning of each word
    B. review the words with the students
    C. imitate the words with the class
    D. model the pronunciation of the words

Answer: C

Explanation: The best way to support English learner is to imitate the words with gesture. This will allow the students to understand the words, but also remember the meanings. Having students look of the meaning or reviewing the words with the students might not be enough for the English learners. The question states "understanding of the words", and option D is related to pronouncing the words.

QUESTION 24

Which of the following changes would be best for a tenth grade student enrolled in a regular classroom who has been diagnosed as having a writing disorder?

    A. give a concrete reinforcement for progressive improvement in handwriting legibility
    B. give the student additional handwriting practice
    C. allow the student to have digital recordings of class lectures and copies of class notes
    D. give the student the opportunity to redo work for improvement purposes

Answer: C

Explanation: The student has been diagnosed with a writing disorder. The best way to support the student is giving the student digital recordings of class lectures and copies of class notes. This will allow the student to focus on the content of the notes as oppose to struggling to write notes.

QUESTION 25

Mr. Barry, a high school teacher, has a goal to develop an effective set of behavior expectations for students, including incentives and consequences. Which of the following guidelines will support Mr. Barry in reaching the goal?

  A. two to four general standards that channel productive learning
  B. five to ten standards that includes detailed information
  C. five to ten standards that define consequences
  D. two to four standards that engages students in doing homework

Answer: A

Explanation: The goal is for students to have effective behavior. In classroom, the students' main goal is to learn. Having two to four general standards that promote productive learning will help Mr. Barry in getting his students to establish an effective set of behavior expectations and a positive learning environment.

QUESTION 26

Which of the following is the best action to take when a student with epilepsy has a seizure?

  A. stay calm and stay with the student until the seizure stops
  B. get the kids out of the room and get help
  C. stay calm, use a tongue suppressor
  D. remove any surrounding objects that can hurt the student

Answer: D

Explanation: As a teacher, the first priority is to ensure the safety of the student, so the best action is to remove surrounding objects that can cause additional harm.

QUESTION 27

Mr. Simon has a great amount of information on students' grade. He does not want to calculate the student's grade every time he is asked about grades. What is the best program he can use to support him?

    A. spreadsheet
    B. database
    C. simulation
    D. model

Answer: A

Explanation: The best tool to use is a spreadsheet for grades. All other options are too advanced for grading purposes.

QUESTION 28

A teacher surveys students about their interests in subject areas; the students' responses matter because they are?

    A. relevant
    B. valid
    C. measurable
    D. consistent

Answer: A

Explanation: The students can fill the survey out randomly without any interest, so the responses are not always valid or consistent. There is no indication that the responses are measurable. The students' interest is relevant to learning.

QUESTION 29

In Mr. Cole's classroom a new student feels unfamiliar. What can Mr. Cole do so the student can feel safe in the classroom?

    A. seat the student near the quietest part of the classroom
    B. seat the student near a group that does not change position
    C. seat the student in the back of the classroom
    D. seat the student in the front of the classroom

Answer: B

Explanation: The student feels unfamiliar, and the question asks for the action that makes the student "feel safe." Having an environment that is the same will support the student in feeling comfortable.

QUESTION 30

Prior to the start of the school year, the principal of a middle school assigns 115 students to a seventh-grade teaching team. The team must then divide the students among the five teachers. Which of the following would be the best approach for the teachers to use in making the groups?

    A. using information from students' records to create groups who are likely to function well together
    B. reviewing students' grades and test scores to create groups of students with alike ability levels
    C. giving students the opportunity on the first day of school to self-select the group
    D. randomly assigning every fifth student from an alphabetical list to the same group

Answer: A

Explanation: Effective groups are best if the group functions well. Using information about students' records allow the teachers to group students that will work together. This will maximize learning.

QUESTION 31

Which activity can a history teacher best use to strengthen tenth-grade students skill in another subject area while developing history knowledge?

    A. playing modern music softly while students complete history paper
    B. request students to write an essay on the theme of Rights and Responsibilities
    C. have students watch a video on the American Revolution and answer multiple choice questions
    D. asking students to read paragraphs from the Declaration of Independence and the Articles of Confederation

Answer: B

Explanation: Option B allows the student to learn the historical theme of Rights and Responsibility as well as engage with English Language Arts.

QUESTION 32

In evaluating a distribution of students' test scores, the mode is determined by identifying the score that:

    A. is earned by the greatest number of times by the students who took the test
    B. represents the average of all scores
    C. is midway between the highest and lowest scores
    D. represents the 30th percentile of all scores in the set of test scores

Answer: A

Explanation: Mode is the number which appears most often in a set of numbers.

QUESTION 33

A high school teacher uses a systematic approach to instruction by giving detailed instructions and requirements for nearly all assignments. Which of the following is a likely consequence of this approach?

    A. maximizing students' learning in the subject area
    B. reducing students' ownership and responsibility in learning
    C. reducing the number of mistakes made by students
    D. having a better ability to see learning patterns

Answer: B

Explanation: Giving detail instructions and requirements will prevent the students from striving to think outside the box, which reduces ownership and responsibility in learning. The students have exactly what they need to do with the instruction and requirements provided by the teacher.

QUESTION 34

A high school science teacher's goal is to get students to follow safety guidelines without constant teacher intervention during experiments. During experiments, the teacher starts by discussing the safety procedures. Which of the following additional approaches would best support the teacher to ensure accomplishment of the goal?

    A. have posters in the classroom about the importance of safety procedures
    B. give the students ample opportunities to implement safety procedures and receive feedback
    C. give extra points for students who follow safety procedures without intervention
    D. establish a buddy system to get peers to support in following safety procedures

Answer: B

Explanation: The goal is to get the student to independently implement safety procedures. To ensure that, the students need ample practice with feedback to ensure procedures are followed automatically and correctly.

QUESTION 35

Matt is a sixth-grade student, and his teacher is having him collect samples of his work for a portfolio. Sample work includes the following:

- artwork
- projects
- graphs
- writing samples

The teacher engages with Matt regularly to assist him in selecting pieces for his portfolio. Which of the following is the main reason for such a portfolio?

    A. support the teacher in assigning report card grades
    B. show parents of the work being done in class
    C. support the student in seeing academic progress
    D. show effectiveness of teaching strategies

Answer: C

Explanation: The student is involved in developing the portfolio, so the student is able to see the progress being made. Portfolios are not developed to support teacher in assigning report card grades. Portfolios can be shown to parents, but that is not the main reason for developing portfolios. The main reason for developing portfolios is not to see the effectiveness of teaching strategies.

QUESTION 36

Mr. Locke, a high school teacher, is teaching a science lesson on the laws of motion. He knows that his students have a natural understanding of the topic going into it. He is intending to understand what they know before he begins the unit. He will use their prior knowledge to create activities to help them understand the physical laws. Which of the following assessments is best for Mr. Locke?

A. criterion-based assessment
B. norms-based assessment
C. formative assessment
D. authentic assessment

Answer: C

Explanation: Mr. Locke is looking to understand prior knowledge to create activity. He can administer a pre-assessment or a diagnostic test, which is within the category of formative assessments.

QUESTION 37

I. coming to school very irritable
II. being hyperactive most of the day
III. fighting with other children

The first step the teacher needs to take in this situation is to:

A. refer the student to the school nurse for deficit/hyperactivity disorder symptoms
B. monitor the behavior for few months to discuss with the principal
C. discuss with parents on home behavior
D. engage with the administrator to develop an intervention plan to support the student

Answer: D

Explanation: The goal is to support the student to prevent the actions that are outlined. To do that, the best approach is to engage with the administrator and develop an intervention plan to support the student.

QUESTION 38

A student and a teacher analyze one novel together by looking at its plot, setting, and characters. Afterward, the teacher asks the student to read three different novels to compare the plots, settings, and characters. What is the objective of this activity?

  A. understand vocabulary
  B. increase reading fluency
  C. promote analytical thinking skills
  D. help students understand the meaning of plot, setting, and character

Answer: C

Explanation: The students are asked to compare the plots, settings, and characters of three novels, so this involves analytical skills. Option A and B are not the answer as there is no indication to promote reading fluency or vocabulary development in this activity. The activity goes beyond understanding plot, setting, and characters as the student is asked to compare.

QUESTION 39

An assistant principal, a principal, and grade level teachers are getting together to discuss math scores to improve scores for the following school year. What kind of meeting are they holding?

  A. school improvement planning
  B. grade level planning
  C. teacher development planning
  D. district improvement planning

Answer: A

Explanation: The assistant principal, a principal, and grade level teachers are looking to improve scores for the next school year, so they are involved in a school improvement planning.

QUESTION 40

Which of the following types of assessments includes a variety of samples of a student's work, collected overtime, that shows the student's growth and development?

    A. anecdotal records
    B. portfolio
    C. running record
    D. grades

Answer: B

Explanation: Portfolios include sample of student's works collected overtime. The portfolios show progression of student's growths and developments.

QUESTION 41

Mr. Mark has a student that has been diagnosed with a disease, and the student will be missing school frequently. The student is in the process of being tested to confirm the prognosis. In class, Mr. Mark's best action to take is:

    A. to observe the student carefully and ask the student frequently if she is doing well
    B. to inform the student that she can go to the nurse at anytime with permission
    C. to send reports to the parents on how the student is doing during class
    D. to assist her in understanding the disease and let her know she has the support of her teacher

Answer: A

Explanation: The student has a disease that can cause complications because the prognosis has not been confirmed. The best action to take is to observe the student and ask the student if she is doing okay. This is a direct impact to supporting the student to ensure action is taken in case something goes wrong. Choice B seems like another possible correct action, but it is not the best approach. Informing the student that she can go to the nurse at anytime is not as impactful as observing the student. Choice C has no direct impact in supporting the student in the classroom. Choice D is not the best option because the teacher may not be qualified to explain the disease.

QUESTION 42

_____ instruction is unambiguous and direct approach to teaching that includes both instructional design and delivery procedures, which includes series of supports or scaffolds, whereby students are guided through the learning process.

    A. Intensive instruction
    B. Indirect instruction
    C. Explicit instruction
    D. Individualized instruction

Answer: C

Explanation: Explicit instruction is unambiguous and direct approach to teaching that includes both instructional design and delivery procedures, which includes series of supports or scaffolds, whereby students are guided through the learning process.

QUESTION 43

    I.   flashcard
    II.   indirect instruction
    III.   paired activity
    IV.   repetition

A middle school reading teacher is having the students read a short story. The teacher starts by having the students develop vocabulary words related to the short story with flashcards. Then, the teacher reads the book out loud while the students listen. After that, the teacher pairs the students, and the teacher has the students read the short story again. Which of the following planned supports did the teacher use in this activity?

    A. I and III
    B. III and IV
    C. I, III, and IV
    D. I, II, III, and IV

Answer: C

Explanation: The planned supports include the flashcards, paired activity, and repetition.

QUESTION 44

A high school teacher is looking to assess the academic achievement of nonnative speakers of English with a standards-based assessment. Which of the following is the most critical aspect of a potential assessment for this purpose?

    A. exam format
    B. free of cultural and linguistic bias
    C. includes common vocabulary words
    D. includes clues to help understand complex questions

Answer: B

Explanation: To ensure fair assessments for nonnative speakers of English, the exam has to be free of cultural and linguistic bias.

QUESTION 45

    I.   a portfolio
    II.   an intelligence test
    III.   an adaptive behavior scale

Of the above, which of the following is/are formal assessment(s)?

    A. I and II
    B. I and III
    C. II and III
    D. I, II, and III

Answer: C

Explanation: A portfolio is an informal assessment. An intelligent test and adaptive behavior scale are formal assessments.

QUESTION 46

Which of the following is the most effective for a teacher to do when making classroom rules?

    A. State the rules ones at the beginning of the school year.
    B. Communicate the rules in an authoritative manner.
    C. Post the rules on the walls of the classroom.
    D. Explain the purpose of rules to better student engagement.

Answer: D

Explanation: When students know the purpose of the rules, the students will remember the rules and more likely follow the rules.

QUESTION 47

An eighth-grade teacher desires to ensure active engagement for students working on an open-ended research question for an English writing paper. The best approach is to use _____.

    A. formal assessments
    B. inquiry-based instruction
    C. indirect instruction
    D. explicit teaching

Answer: B

Explanation: Inquiry-based learning is dealing with posing questions, problems, or scenarios instead of just presenting established facts or portraying a smooth path to knowledge. Inquiry-based instruction involves active engagement and is a good approach with when working with open-ended research questions.

QUESTION 48

More than 70% of a 3rd-grade class scored at high risk on the oral reading fluency. Which instructional practice would be best for improving the students' oral reading fluency?

    A. having students independently read
    B. having students participate in round-robin reading
    C. having students repeat readings of familiar text with corrective feedback
    D. having students do a paired-reading activity

Answer: C

Explanation: Oral reading fluency is the ability to translate letters to sounds and sounds to words. Majority of the students need support in oral reading fluency, so the best approach is to have students read and reread along with providing feedback. The feedback will allow the student to improve the skill.

QUESTION 49

In gym class, James is unable to walk across a balance beam. Which of the following is the best option to undertake?

    A. place tape next to the beam and have him walk on the tape
    B. defer activity to the latter part of the year
    C. have him write how others completed activity
    D. have him watch video of kids walking across a balance beam

Answer: A

Explanation: Choice A is the only option that provides direct support in the gym and can support the student in accomplishing the task. Choice B is not the best option as no intervention is undertaken. Choice C is likely going to make the child feel uncomfortable as he will see others can do the activity and he can't. Watching a video is more for awareness purposes of walking on balance beam and that stage has passed; he attempted to walk but was unsuccessful. He needs intervention to support him in walking across the balance beam.

QUESTION 50

A teacher starts developing a lesson plan by deciding the instructional outcomes. The most appropriate next step for the teacher to take in planning the lesson is to determine

    A. the activities that should be included.

    B. the assessment type for the activity.

    C. the resources required in the lesson.

    D. if the outcome is realistic for the grade level.

Answer: D

Explanation: To ensure learning of the students, a teacher must develop outcomes that are realistic for the grade level. After deciding the instructional outcomes, the next step is to check if the outcomes are realistic.

QUESTION 51

An ESL teacher teaches beginning-level English Language Learners conversational techniques such as elaboration and circumlocution. To allow students to apply the techniques, the teacher has the students practice these strategies in conversations with partners at different English proficiency levels. The teacher's instructional method primarily allows the students' to develop by

    A. increasing relationship with classmates.

    B. giving opportunity to produce logical language output.

    C. allowing students to see different levels of English proficiency.

    D. giving students opportunity to apply knowledge.

Answer: B

Explanation: The teacher is having the students work with partners at different English levels. The students will communicate with each other, allowing them to produce logical language output.

QUESTION 52

Which of the following best represents a commitment from teachers, parents, and students to work together to support student learning?

    A. parent teacher conference

    B. learning contract

    C. progress report

    D. letter informing expectations

Answer: B

Explanation: The keyword in the question is commitment. To establish commitment, a learning contract is the best approach. The student, parents, and teacher will sign the contract that outlines the expectations. A letter is used for information purposes, so D is not the correct option. Parent teacher conference does not involve the student, so A is not the correct option. Progress report does not establish a commitment, so C is not the right answer.

QUESTION 53

Which statement would be classified as a long term goal rather than a course or lesson objective?

  A. The student will analyze independently informational text.
  B. The student will be able to identify the verbs in a paragraph.
  C. The student will be able to develop a well organized presentation.
  D. The student will be able to identify main ideas.

Answer: A

Explanation: Analyzing independently is a skill that will take some time to develop , so this is consider a long term goal.

QUESTION 54

Daryl is concerned about one of his eleventh grade student who has missed many school days recently. When Daryl approached the student with his concern, the student informed him that school was not worth going to and saw no need to pursue school so he was working at a part-time restaurant. In order to understand the student's perspective, Daryl needs to have which development knowledge to pursue forward in an effective dialogue?

  A. The student may have financial difficulties at home.
  B. The student may not have any concern for the future and is more concerned with the present.
  C. The student is likely still operating at the operational stage of thinking process.
  D. Students at this age typically place more focus on peer modeling.

Answer: B

Explanation: Based on the situation, the student is more concerned about the present as opposed to the future. In the question, it states "school was not worth going to." The student does not understand the long term impact of school. The student needs to understand the impact school has on an individual's future.

QUESTION 55

A ninth grade teacher has her students participate in a series of debates on school related topics. Topics include dress code and afterschool programs. This activity is related to ninth grade student mostly because students at this age have typically developed the ability to

    A. establish good communication skills to debate.
    B. perceive different perspectives on issues.
    C. think at higher level.
    D. engage in formal operational thinking.

Answer: B

Explanation: At the ninth grade level, students develop the ability to see different positions. Communication skills (Option A) and critical thinking skills (Option C) are developed before the ninth grade.

QUESTION 56

A teacher is planning to organize study teams for the entire school year in order for students to support other students. Prior to assigning the groups, the teacher undertakes the following:

    1. Observes students interaction in various team activities
    2. Gives some homework and grade the homework
    3. Gives explicit instructions on how study teams function

The approach taken by the teacher in developing study team is expected to benefit the student most by:

    A. having groups organized to ensure no one student is working more than the other
    B. establishing a network of peers who can support one another
    C. increasing communication and collaborating skills
    D. increase student attention and seriousness of school

Answer: B

Explanation: The keywords in the questions are entire "school year", "support students", and "benefit". The teacher is establishing a network of peers to support one another. Option A, C, and D does not relate to the impact of establishing study teams.

QUESTION 57

A high school physics teacher is on the lesson of velocity and acceleration. The teacher has done the following to convey information to the students:

- discussed relevant sections from textbook
- created diagrams to explain the concepts
- shown videos on velocity and acceleration applications in science

After completing the above, the students are still having difficulty understanding the concept related to velocity and acceleration. Which of the following is the most appropriate to undertake next to assist in students' understanding these concepts?

    A. explain basics behind velocity and acceleration
    B. repeat the information, but take breaks to ask questions for understanding
    C. provide students with examples of the concepts related to their own experiences
    D. perform experiments that explain velocity and acceleration

Answer: C

Explanation: Examples are important to support students in understanding concepts. More importantly, having examples connected to real experiences increase the chances of students' understanding concepts.

QUESTION 58

An eighth-grade teacher is going to have her class undertake an individual research project in which students will be required to write a paper on a self-selected topic. Later, he teacher decides to have students complete the research paper in small groups. Which of the following is a reason explaining why the group approach is going to be most effective for eighth-grade students?

    A. increase participation as students will be able to communicate with peers in learning process
    B. increase students' interests as work will be distributed
    C. allow students to complete detailed and complex research in groups
    D. give students opportunity to learn from other students on unfamiliar topics

Answer: A

Explanation: Group activities increase participation as students engage with peers. Peer engagement is critical at the middle school/high school level in the learning process. This is a research paper on a self-selected topic, so the students will pick a topic that is interesting to them, which eliminates answer choice B. The complexity of the research is not changed just because the paper is being done in groups. Choice D is a good option, but it is into the reason that makes it the most effective.

QUESTION 59

A teacher has been working at a school for three months. After evaluating the needs of the district, the teacher has been informed that she will have to go to another school. The teacher refuses this move, and she takes action to abandon the position without in advance notification. The teacher has:

    A. inappropriately abandon the position
    B. the right to abandon the position
    C. taken appropriate action
    D. breached the contract

Answer: D

Explanation: The contracts of teachers indicate that an advanced notification is required prior to leaving teaching positions. Moreover, common practice is to give an advanced notification, so the school can make arrangements for temporary or permanent replacement.

QUESTION 60

A teacher is seeking to find out if students have mastered the instructional objectives at the end of the unit. What type of assessment is the best to use?

    A. norm referenced
    B. achievement
    C. diagnostic
    D. placement

Answer: B

Explanation: An achievement test is a test of developed skill or knowledge.

QUESTION 61

In a middle school classroom, a student is constantly distracting students during silent reading. From the standpoint of logical consequence approach to classroom management, which of the following is the best action for the teacher to take?

    A. place the student to an individual work station during silent reading
    B. remind him that there will be consequences for interruptions
    C. have the student hear the teacher during silent reading
    D. assign a buddy to help the student stay on track

Answer: A

Explanation: The question states "logical consequence approach", so there has to be some type of consequence associated with the misbehavior. Placing the student at an individual work station during silent reading will serve as a consequence that will also be effective in promoting positive behavior.

QUESTION 62

Which of the following instructional strategies best completes the chart?

Reading Comprehension	Reading Fluency	Writing	Vocabulary
Think-Pair-Share	Readers' theater	Revision	Word walls
Direct Reading-Thinking	?	Sentence combining	Word hunts
Inquiry chart	Partner reading	Paragraph hamburger	Possible sentence

    A. Shared reading
    B. Brainstorming
    C. Anticipation guide
    D. Guided reading

Answer: A

Explanation: The best answer is shared reading. The other options do not connect with direct reading-thinking.

QUESTION 63

The Family Educational Rights and Privacy Act of 1974 give parents/guardians of a minor who is getting special needs services the right to:

    A. remove their child from standardize exams
    B. obtain educational records to share with non-school individuals
    C. select special education services
    D. opt out of IEP meetings

Answer: B

Explanation: The Family Educational Rights and Privacy Act of 1974 give parents or guardians of a minor to obtain copies of students' academic records to share with individuals outside of the school system.

QUESTION 64

IDEA covers which of the following disabilities from birth:

    I.   cerebral palsy
    II.   visual impairment
   III. Down syndrome
   IV. hearing impairment

    A. I and III
    B. II and IV
    C. I and II
    D. III and IV

Answer: A

Explanation: Cerebral palsy and Down syndrome are conditions that cause severe learning disabilities and cognitive developmental issues. Cerebral palsy and Down syndrome are covered from birth under IDEA.

QUESTION 65

What is one way a teacher can avoid confusion and delays caused by activity transitions?

    A. increase voice during transitions to ensure everyone is listening
    B. establish a daily schedule with clear objectives
    C. ask students to stop all work and put down their pencils
    D. provide incentives for timely transitions

Answer: B

Explanation: Having clear objectives and a schedule will support in time management and transition of activities. Giving incentives is not a long term solution, so Choice D is eliminated. Abruptly stopping all work will not always be the best approach, so Choice C is eliminated. Choice A does not directly solve the confusion and delays due to activity transitions.

QUESTION 66

Interactive writing between the student and the teacher is:

    A. dialogue journal
    B. essay writing
    C. social network
    D. unethical

Answer: A

Explanation: A dialogue journal is a daily written dialogue between the educator and the student.

QUESTION 67

A student doesn't understand very well what the teacher is explaining. The teacher realizes that the student is having hearing loss. What kind of assistive technology can the teacher use to help the student with the problem?

    A. visuals
    B. gestures
    C. text-to-voice technology
    D. speech-to-text technology

Answer: D

Explanation: In this situation, the teacher is explaining verbally, and the student is having difficulty. So, technology that converts speech to text is needed to support the student.

QUESTION 68

A reporter is interested about the social activities that a student is involved within a high school club, and asks the teacher about the student. The teacher should:

    A. tell the reporter that the student is enrolled
    B. report to the principal
    C. invite the reporter to the school
    D. not tell the reporter anything regarding the student

Answer: D

Explanation: Giving information about students to reporters (or third party) is against school policy.

QUESTION 69

Which of the following assessments is used to evaluate student learning at the conclusion of an instructional period (ex. at the end of a unit)?

    A. formative assessment
    B. interim assessment
    C. summative assessment
    D. placement assessment

Answer: C

Explanation: Summative assessment is used to evaluate student learning at the conclusion of an instructional period. Formative assessment is an in-process evaluation of learning that is normally administered multiple times during a unit or course. Placement assessment is used to place students in courses. Interim assessment is used to see if students are in the right track for learning.

QUESTION 70

A classroom teacher consults with another teacher regarding the best approach for meeting the needs of a culturally different student who is about to enter the class. Which of the following would be the most appropriate advice?

    A. reward students in the class who assist the new student.
    B. adhere to current instructional programs and standards
    C. provide the student with instruction in the social and cultural values of the United States
    D. investigate the student's culture to improve understanding of cultural differences to improve learning

Answer: D

Explanation: Having understanding of the student's culture will allow the teacher to interact with the student better and allow the teacher to tailor lesson to the student's needs.

QUESTION 71

A student panics during a fire drill and runs out of the classroom. What approach could the teacher implement to stop this from happening in the future?

    A. show a video of fire drill procedures and safety rules
    B. practice role playing a fire drill situation; practicing rules and procedures
    C. have a discussion about rules and procedures of fire drills
    D. explain the procedures for a fire drill and have the student write the procedures

Answer: B

Explanation: Having the student practice via role playing supports the student in acting properly during a fire drill.

QUESTION 72

Parents come to school and want to see their child's records. The teacher should inform the parents that:

    A. they need to make an appointment to see records
    B. records are confidential and cannot be shown to anyone
    C. allow them to see the child's records
    D. have them discuss the request with the principal

Answer: C

Explanation: Parents are allowed to see their child's academic records.

QUESTION 73

Which of the following is the best to use when deciding whether or not the students are ready for the next content?

    A. survey students to determine if they are ready to move to the next content area
    B. review progress reports and report cards
    C. review previous standardized tests
    D. administer entrance tests

Answer: D

Explanation: Entrance tests will be the best option to see if the students have the background knowledge to move into the next content area.

QUESTION 74

A 55% percentile rank means what?

    A. 55% of questions correct
    B. below 55%
    C. above 55%
    D. 55% better than the rest of the kids

Answer: B

Explanation: A percentile rank is the percentage of scores that fall at or below a given score.

QUESTION 75

High school teachers meet frequently to discuss strategies to support students struggling in science. Which of the following is the main benefit of their meetings?

    A. gives opportunity to support all students
    B. provides different instructional methods
    C. provides professional development
    D. eliminates poor practices and fosters positive practices

Answer: A

Explanation: The teachers meet to discuss how to support students who are struggling. By doing so, the meetings give opportunity to support all students in learning.

QUESTION 76

Mrs. Barbara is seeking to teach listening skills to her early childhood students. What is the best approach for her to take?

    A. play a guessing game
    B. call on students not participating
    C. reading different stories and having the students answer questions about the story
    D. state a list of nonsense words and have the students repeat them back

Answer: D

Explanation: Choice D requires students to recite words that were communicated to them; this involves listening skills. Choice C involves listening skills, but is more targeted toward comprehension skills.

QUESTION 77

Kate focuses better in the morning. How can Kate's teacher better instruct her?

    A. direct instruction needs to be done in the afternoon
    B. direct instruction needs to be done in the morning
    C. complete group activities in the morning
    D. teach only in the morning

Answer: B

Explanation: Direct instruction requires the student to be completely focused. If the student is focused other in the morning, the best approach is to do direct instruction in the morning.

QUESTION 78

The school sent out a notice not to bring lunches with peanut butter. Jake, a middle-grade student, who has brought a peanut butter sandwich for lunch. The teacher saw the sandwich immediately, when Jake took it out of his lunch box. What should the teacher do first?

    A. call the school nurse in case someone has an allergic reaction
    B. take the sandwich and throw it in a trash basket away from the students
    C. have Jake sit away from the students to eat his sandwich
    D. call Jake's parents to remind him to not bring lunch with peanut butter

Answer: B

Explanation: The first step is to protect the students, so the teacher will want to throw the sandwich away.

QUESTION 79

Mr. Raymond has seen that John, who is claustrophobic, has been the last person to turn in-class assignment 12 times in a row. His grades on the assignments are above average. What is the likely reason for John being the last person to turn in assignments?

    A. He double checks his work.
    B. He is shy to come up to the front.
    C. He does not want to come upfront while everyone else is turning in assignments.
    D. He is afraid someone might push him.

Answer: C

Explanation: John is claustrophobic, so going into crowded areas will be difficult for him. He is not going to want to come upfront while everyone is turning in assignments.

QUESTION 80

    I.   all special education students in America
    II.   students with severe disabilities
    III. students eligible for special education in public schools

IEP is/are required for:

A. I only
B. I and II
C. II and III
D. I, II, and III

Answer: C

Explanation: Students in private schools are not mandated to have IEPs, which eliminates options that include I.

QUESTION 81

For the last two weeks, a teacher has been abruptly ending lessons as she is unable to finish teaching. The best approach is to:

A. decrease the length of the lesson activity
B. increase the speed of teaching
C. have students ask questions at the very end
D. find a way to end the lessons in a smooth manner even if the lessons are not completed

Answer: D

Explanation: Lessons can go over the allotted time. Teachers should not abruptly end the lesson as it can have a negative impact. The best option is to end the lesson in a smooth manner.

QUESTION 82

Which of the following is the best listening comprehension content for English Learners who have mastered basic structural forms but not vocabulary development?

    A. vocabulary words to memorize
    B. oral readings with accompanying pictures
    C. television shows
    D. flashcards

Answer: B

Explanation: The question asks for listening skills, so A and D are eliminated. Television shows are not the best way to develop vocabulary words, so C is eliminated. The best way is to do oral reading and have pictures to help understand vocabulary words.

QUESTION 83

Jake, a high school math teacher, is teaching one student the entire day. Blair, a general education teacher, has observed that Jake is doing nothing to teach the student. The first action for Blair to undertake is:

    A. confront the teacher and inform the teacher to do his job
    B. inform the school principal
    C. open dialogue to see what Jake has done and continue to observe
    D. inform Jake that he can ask for support

Answer: C

Explanation: The best approach is to open dialogue to see what he has done and continue to observe to get an idea if he is really working to support the student, and continue to observe. Going immediately to the principal or directly confronting Jake might result in a negative environment. After continuing to observe Jake, if the concerns are not addressed, Jake can take actions to involve other administrators.

QUESTION 84

_____ are assessments that provide information on where an individual student's performance is in relation to his/her peers.

    A. Formative assessments
    B. Norm-referenced assessments
    C. Criterion-referenced assessments
    D. Subjective assessments

Answer: B

Explanation: Norm-referenced assessments are assessments that provide information on where an individual student's performance is in relation to his or her peers.

QUESTON 85

    I.   be informed of specific charges
    II.   have character witnesses during punishment phase
    III.   have their case be heard at the district level

Students who are facing suspension for actions that violate school rules have the right to:

    A. I only
    B. I and II
    C. II and III
    D. I, II, and III

Answer: A

Explanation: When students are facing suspension, they have the right to know about the specific charges. Character witness is not a right and neither is having the case heard at the district level.

QUESTION 86

Which of the following would be best for preparing students on taking standardized tests?

    A. Teach test-taking skills from the beginning of the year as part of regular instruction.
    B. Prior to two-three months of examination, teach test-taking skills as part of regular instruction.
    C. Devote one day of the week to teach test-taking skills.
    D. Subject area teachers should teach test-taking skills to all students.

Answer: B

Explanation: The best answer is to teach test-taking skills 2-3 months prior to the standardized exam, so students can remember the skills. Teaching test-taking skills from the beginning of the school or one day a week goes beyond expectations.

QUESTION 87

Which technique is most effective in promoting a ninth grade teacher's expectations for assignments?

    A. keeping a list of due dates for each assignment for the grade period
    B. maintaining a list of assignments due for each 9 week grading period
    C. requiring parent's signature on each assignment
    D. posting a grading rubrics for each assignment

Answer: D

Explanation: A teacher's expectation for assignments can be well communicated by a rubric.

QUESTION 88

A middle school teacher is looking to use an informal assessment to capture overall learning. Which of the following is the best option?

    A. authentic assessment
    B. graded homework
    C. exit card
    D. performance assessment

Answer: C

Explanation: Of the answer choices, only an exit card is an informal assessment.

QUESTION 89

Cole, a seventh-grade student with ADHD, is not happy with his grade and is loudly communicating that to his teacher. What is the best action for the teacher to take?

    A. re-grade the assignment
    B. explain to the student what he got incorrect, so he can prevent the same mistakes in the future
    C. allow him to retake the assignment
    D. inform the student there will be more opportunities to improve

Answer: B

Explanation: The best approach is to have the teacher explain the questions he got wrong, so he can to prevent similar mistakes in the future. Choice A and C are clearly not the best options as they are unfair to other students. Choice D seems like a good choice, but, for students with ADHD, the teacher needs to spend more time engaging instead of informing the student there will be more opportunities to improve.

QUESTION 90

_____ score is a measurement concept that compares a student's test performance with those of other students of the same grade level?

A. Scaled
B. Developmental
C. Standard
D. Average

Answer: C

Explanation: Standard scores are a measurement concept that compare a student's test performance with those of other students of the same grade level

QUESTION 91

Carla is the mother of Susan, who attends middle school. Susan has come home multiple times with scratches inflicted by another student, Martha. Which of the following best indicates the most inappropriate response for the teacher to undertake along with what action the teacher should undertake?

A. The teacher would be wrong to tell the parent that Martha and Susan had difficulty working together that day. The teacher would be right in informing the parent that she will monitor both students closely going forward and report back.

B. The teacher would be wrong to generalize that there might have been some provocative verbal communication, which resulted in the scratches. The teacher would be right to take action by involving the principal and recommending appropriate punishments.

C. The teacher would be wrong to suggest that Martha's action resulted due to issues occurring in her family. The teacher would be right in informing the parent that she will monitor both students closely going forward and report back.

D. The teacher would be wrong to generalize that there might have been some provocative verbal communication, which resulted in the scratches. The teacher would be right in informing the parent that she will monitor both students closely going forward and report back.

Answer: C

Explanation: The teacher does not have the knowledge of the family to suggest the scratches were due to issues occurring in the student's family. The teacher needs to monitor both students closely and report further issues.

QUESTION 92

Mary, a middle school teacher, is alarmed by one student's appearance and behavior as the perceptions seems that she has been physically abused at home. According to state and federal law, the teacher is required to immediately:

A. inform the school nurse to allow him or her to take appropriate action
B. ensure her suspicions are reported in compliance with state/federal law requirements
C. contact the parents to inform them of the situation
D. ask indirect questions to confirm suspicions and proceed in contacting law enforcement

Answer: B

Explanation: State and federal law require that suspicion of child abuse be reported to appropriate agencies. The teacher has suspected abuse and it is required for the teacher to report the suspicions, so necessary individuals can investigate.

QUESTION 93

Family Educational Rights and Privacy Action (FERPA) protect students' records at school institutions in America. Which of the following situations of a request to see a student's records will be approved?

A. A parent seeking to confirm a student's enrollment in the appropriate special education program.
B. A parent seeking to confirm a student's IEP is acceptable to ensure proper learning.
C. A parent questioning a student's placement for special education classes for the new school year.
D. A parent questioning a student's grades and requesting to see all assignment grades.

Answer: C

Explanation: Choice A does not require the need for academic records nor has anything to do with FERPA. Choice B is incorrect as IEP are provided and discussed with parents; FERPA does not address this. Choice C is correct as that is acceptable reason to view records. Choice D is incorrect as FERPA does not go into details about parents challenging student's grades.

QUESTION 94

A teacher notices a student removing food from lunch and hiding it in his backpack. The teacher notices this behavior and discusses it with the student after class. In the discussion, the student mentions his father lost his job and that there is not much food to eat. Which of the following is the most appropriate first response for the teacher to take?

    A. contact the principal to develop a plan to ensure proper food is given to the student outside of the school
    B. contact Child Protective Services (CPS) to report possible neglect at home
    C. provide the student with food and snacks to take home going forward
    D. speak to the family about relevant community services and support during this difficult time

Answer: D

Explanation: The best action to take is to talk to the family and inform them of the support systems available. At this time, escalating this to the principal and CPS is unnecessary. Providing the student with food and snacks is not the right direction to proceed in.

QUESTION 95

A student brings a gift to school for his teacher. The best action for the teacher is to refuse the gift if:

    A. the gift is expensive
    B. the gift would affect student-teacher relationship
    C. the student's parents are unaware
    D. the student's gift is cheap

Answer: B

Explanation: The gift needs to be refused if the relationship is impacted in any way due to the student providing the gift.

QUESTION 96

Several ninth-grade students are doing well in math class, but they are having difficulty on tests and quizzes, what should their teacher do?

    A. find out their study habits and find lessons to support the students
    B. plan a unit on study habits
    C. see if there are patterns on the questions students are getting wrong
    D. do review sessions before tests and quizzes

Answer: A

Explanation: Students are doing well in class, but struggling on the quizzes and tests. This is indication that the students are likely not studying correctly. The best option is for the teacher to find out about their study habits and support them in studying the correct way.

QUESTION 97

Juan is an eighth grade student. Coming to class every day is very important for his success in learning. The teacher notices that Juan has missed class every Thursday for the last four weeks. What is the best action for the teacher to take?

    A. ask Juan what he does on Thursday
    B. call his parents to discuss the absences
    C. have someone track Juan on Thursday
    D. tell Juan that missing class on any Thursday is unacceptable

Answer: B

Explanation: The best approach is to call Juan's parents and discuss the absences. In particular, discuss the pattern noticed. Inform the parents of the consequences of students being absent constantly.

QUESTION 98

To prevent common cold and the flu within schools, a teacher can

    A. have students wash hands properly and frequently throughout the day
    B. have students not work in group activities
    C. discourage sharing food
    D. keep tissues near each students' desks

Answer: A

Explanation: Properly washing hands is important to reduce spreading common cold and the flu. Students interact in schools, so Choice A has a larger impact on preventing/reducing common cold and the flu.

QUESTION 99

The purpose of putting severely handicapped students in a general education classroom is to:

    A. teach life skills
    B. teach academic skills
    C. teach same lessons
    D. teach social skills

Answer: D

Explanation: All children need to interact in society. One of the purposes of having a severely handicapped student in a general education classroom is for the student to develop social skills.

QUESTION 100

James is student with a Functional Behavioral Assessment (FBA). He has unexpectedly become physically aggressive with others in school. To ensure effective intervention, which of the following should be done first by the IEP team?

  A. interview peers and teachers
  B. define behavior in measureable terms
  C. predict reasoning for changes in behavior
  D. develop a plan to collect data

Answer: B

Explanation: Having the behavior defined in measurable terms will allow concrete information when evaluating effectiveness of the intervention plan.

Constructed Response 1

Use the information below to complete the task that follows.

Mr. Barry is a sixth-grade math teacher whose fifth-period class includes 30 students. The class includes five students who have been identified as gifted and two students with cognitive impairment.

Mr. Barry is moving into doing advance mathematics related to operations. He is reviewing previous assessments and records of all students related to performing basic operations (addition, subtraction, multiplication, and division), which results in answers of 450 or greater.

Assessment Records – Summary			
	Score Range (% correct)	**Mean Score**	**Median Score**
Single Operations			
Addition	78-95	84	74
Subtraction	74-95	85	73
Multiplication	73-97	84	75
Division	74-95	83	73
Multiple Operations			
Addition/Subtraction	56-76	60	62
Addition/Division	63-77	70	68
Division/Multiplication	53-59	54	54
Multiplication/Subtraction	53-60	54	54

Citing evidence from the information provided, write a response in which you:

- identify one specific learning need related to the planned lesson for students in Mr. Barry's class;
- describe one strategy for differentiating instruction in the planned lesson to address the identified need; and
- explain why the strategy you described would be effective in addressing the identified need.

Response: Use email tutoring services to send constructed response to obtain detail feedback and scores.

Constructed Response 2

Use the information below to complete the task that follows.

Mr. Martin, a sixth-grade reading teacher, has a classroom with 30 heterogeneously grouped students ages 13 to 15. The teacher is looking to start the lesson on reading factual texts. In particular, the teacher is looking to do cross curriculum lesson in which the teacher will have students read text related to World War II. Below includes information on three of Mr. Martin's students.

Student 1 – Alex
- came to America roughly one year ago
- nonnative speaker of English
- unable to respond to questions with confidence
- misspells words constantly
- barely communicates with classmates

Student 2 – Lila
- unexpectedly becomes aggressive with others
- reads at a fourth grade level
- recently diagnosed with ADHD
- always unhappy with her grade
- distracting other students

Student 3 – Jasper
- mild form of dyslexia
- recently been told by doctor to wear glasses
- fails to turn in assignments on time
- shy to answer questions in discussion
- has test anxiety

Citing evidence from the information provided, write a response in which you:

- Identify two learning supports Mr. Martin can use to support all three learners.
- Explain how the learning supports helps each of the student in learning.

Response: Use email tutoring services to send constructed response to obtain detail feedback and scores.

This page is intentionally left blank.

NES® Assessment of Professional Knowledge Secondary
National Evaluation Series™

Made in the USA
San Bernardino, CA
21 November 2017